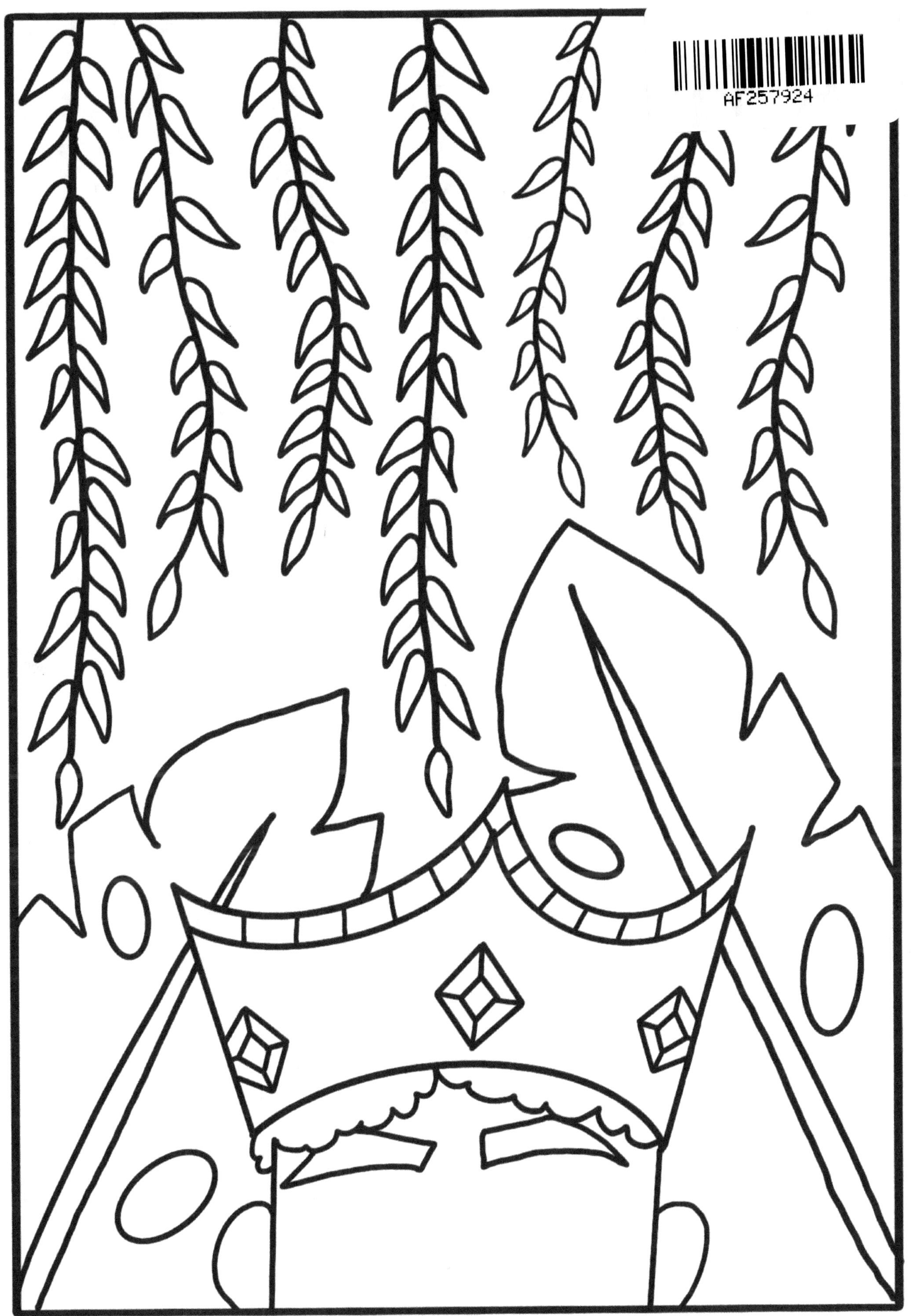
AF257924

Published by
Revolutionary Hearts Industries
Illustrated by Naomi Winston

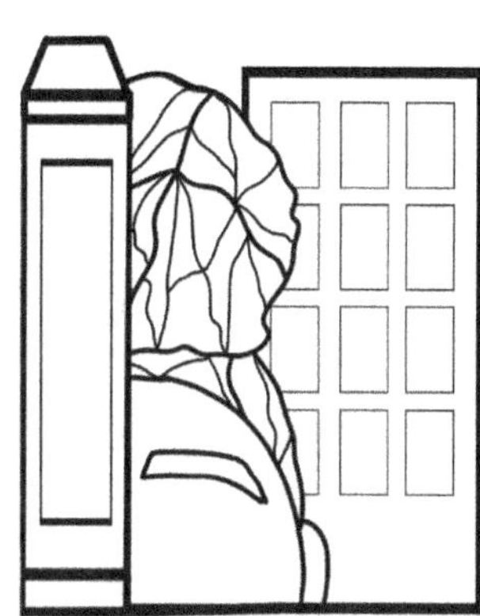

To an amazing human being,

Firstly, I want to say that you are such an important part of this world. I hope that this coloring book is able to help you set the goals that you have for your own future.

I want to say that your future is incredibly bright and I have all the faith in the world that you can not only achieve EVERY single goal that you have but also that you are a person who is capable of doing whatever you want to in life.

Please use this coloring book throughout the year to look back at your goals. I was always told that writing my goals down made me 10x more likely to achieve them.

You will do everything you have ever dreamed.
You will achieve your goals.
You will flourish.

I have faith in you.
I care about you.
I believe in you.

Don't forget that everything has a purpose, and you are everything!

LETTER FROM THE AUTHOR

YOU ARE THE FUTURE

Who am I?
Draw Yourself

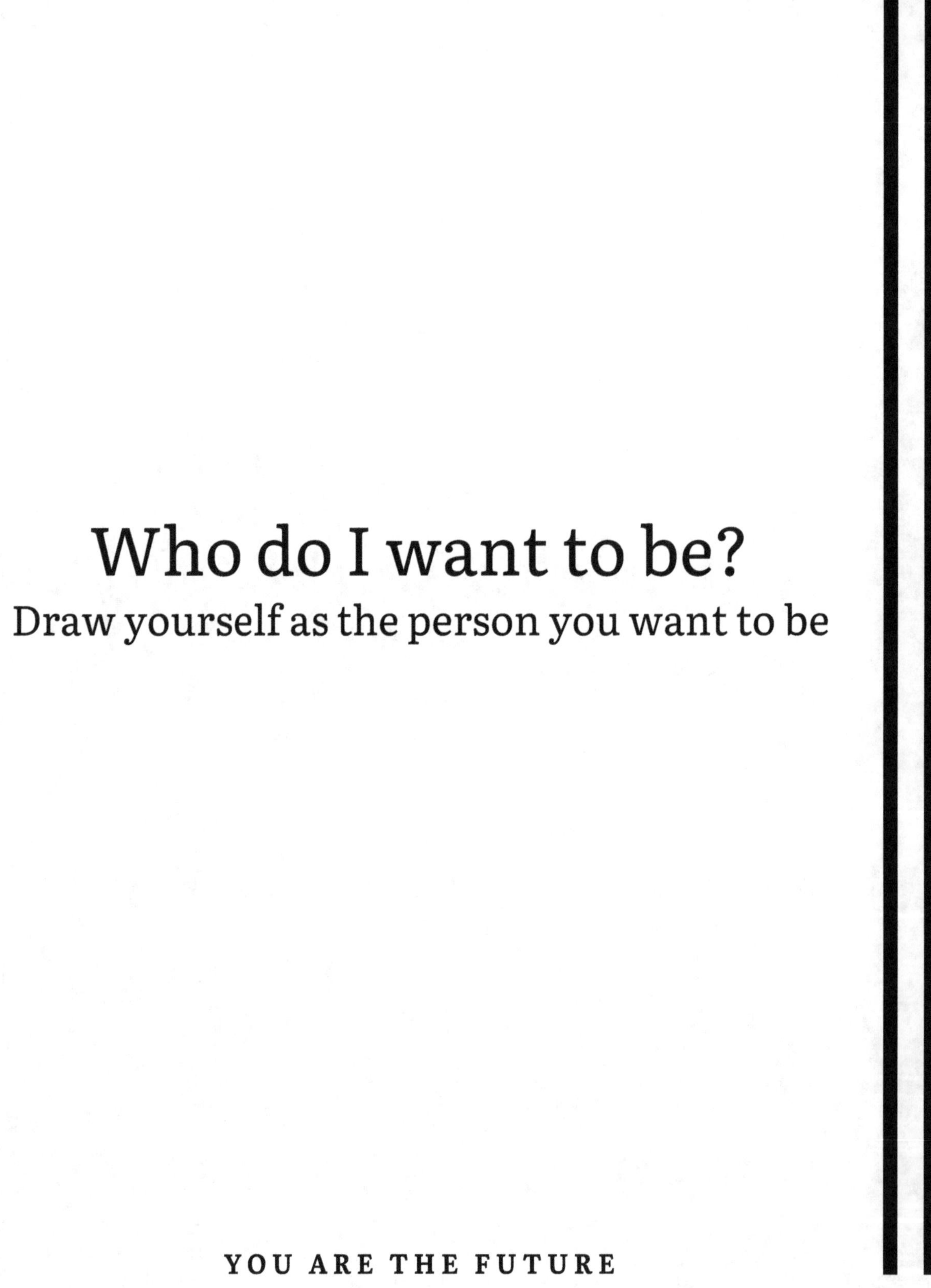

Who do I want to be?
Draw yourself as the person you want to be

YOU ARE THE FUTURE

What makes me happy?

Draw Yourself doing what makes you happy.

Writing down your goals is
important because it
increases the chance you will
achieve them.

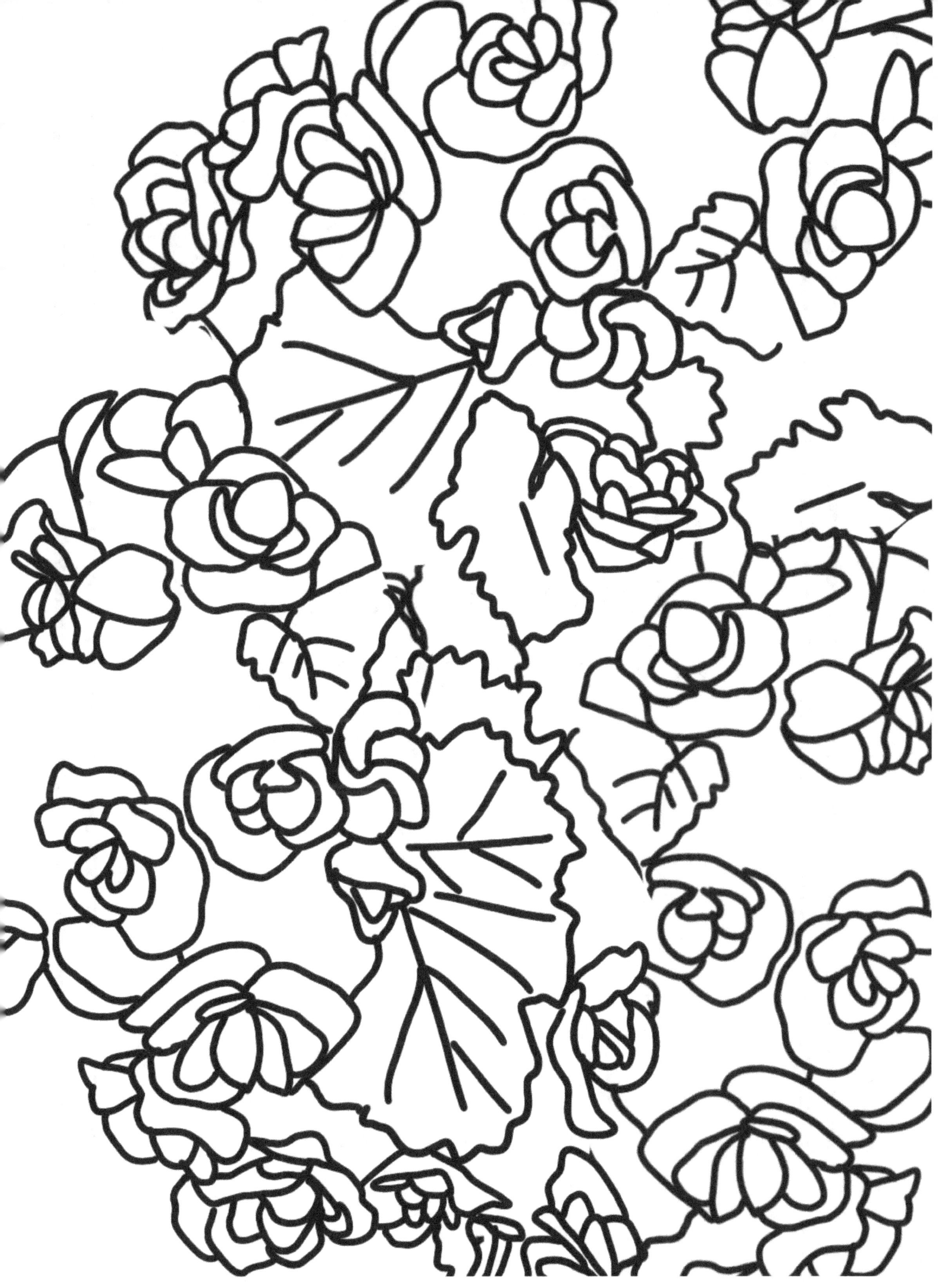

What do I want to accomplish this year?

What do I want to accomplish this year?

What are my goals?

What are my goals?

What is something I want to learn this year?

What is something I want to learn this year?

What is one thing I can do everyday to make the world better?

We will create a plan together to help you achieve your goals.

What is one thing I can do everyday to make the world better?

Affirmations are words that you can say to yourself whenever you feel sad or when you want to be nice to yourself.

You deserve to be nice to yourself.

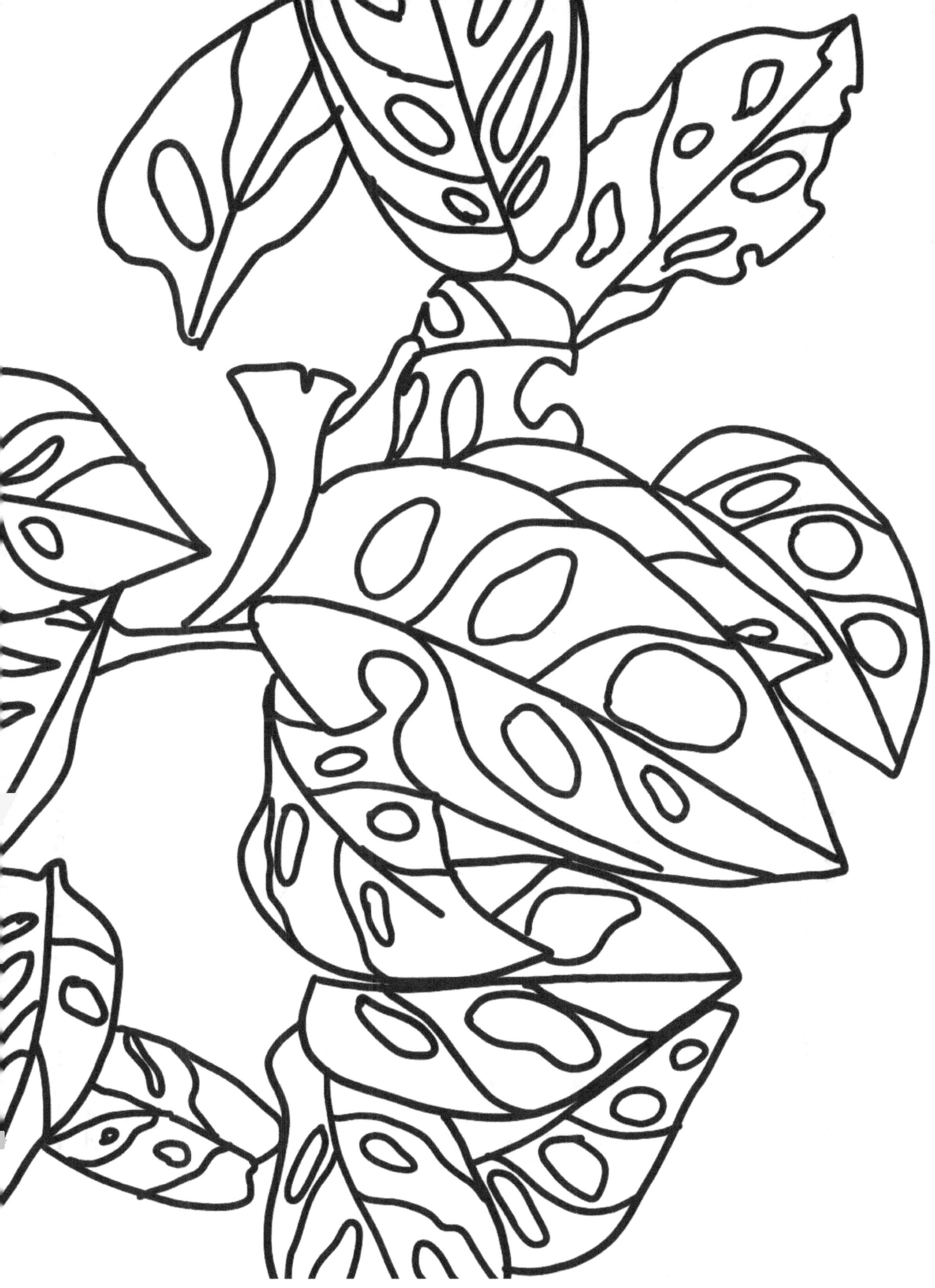

I am kind

YOU ARE THE FUTURE

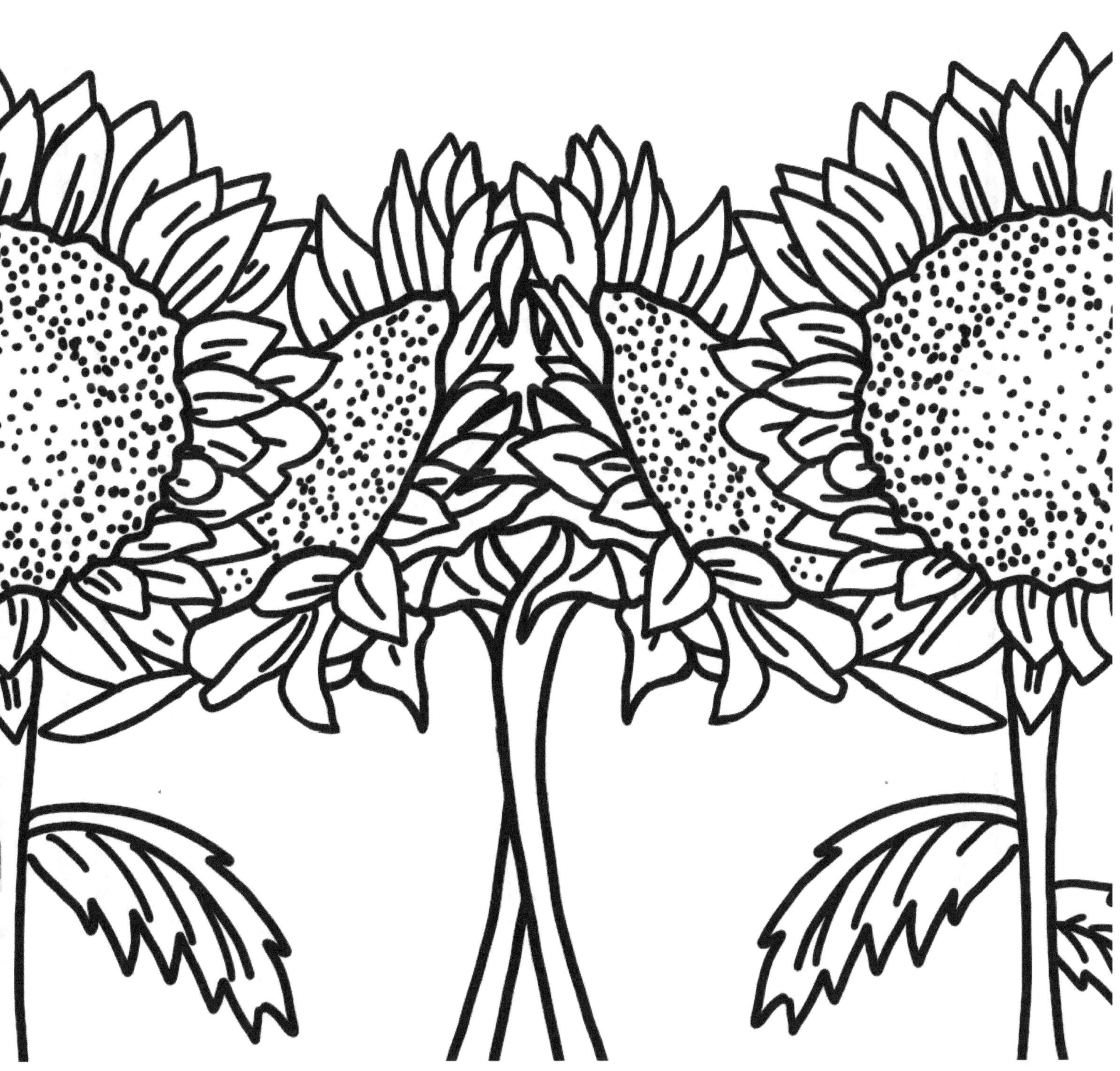

I am good

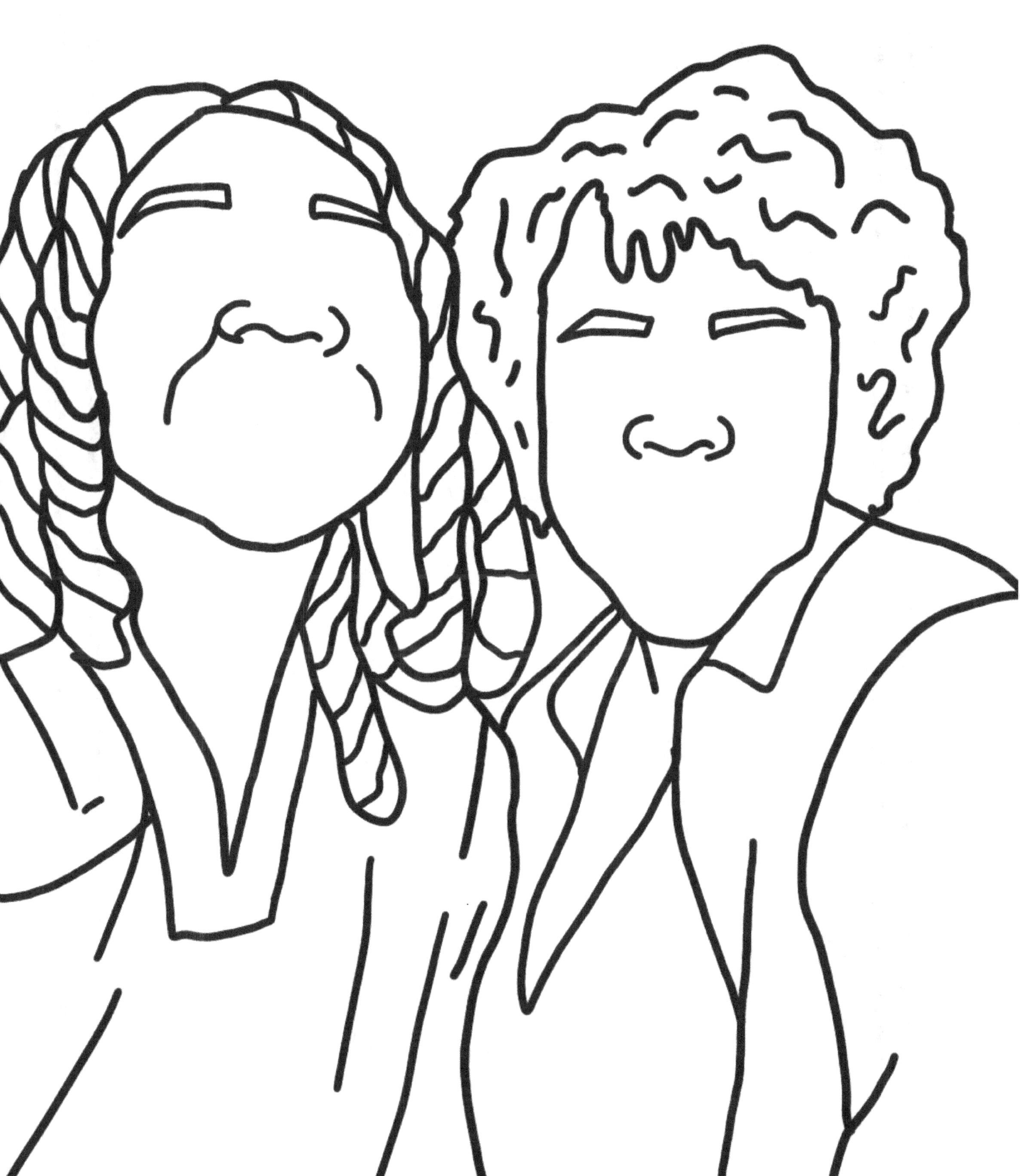

I have purpose

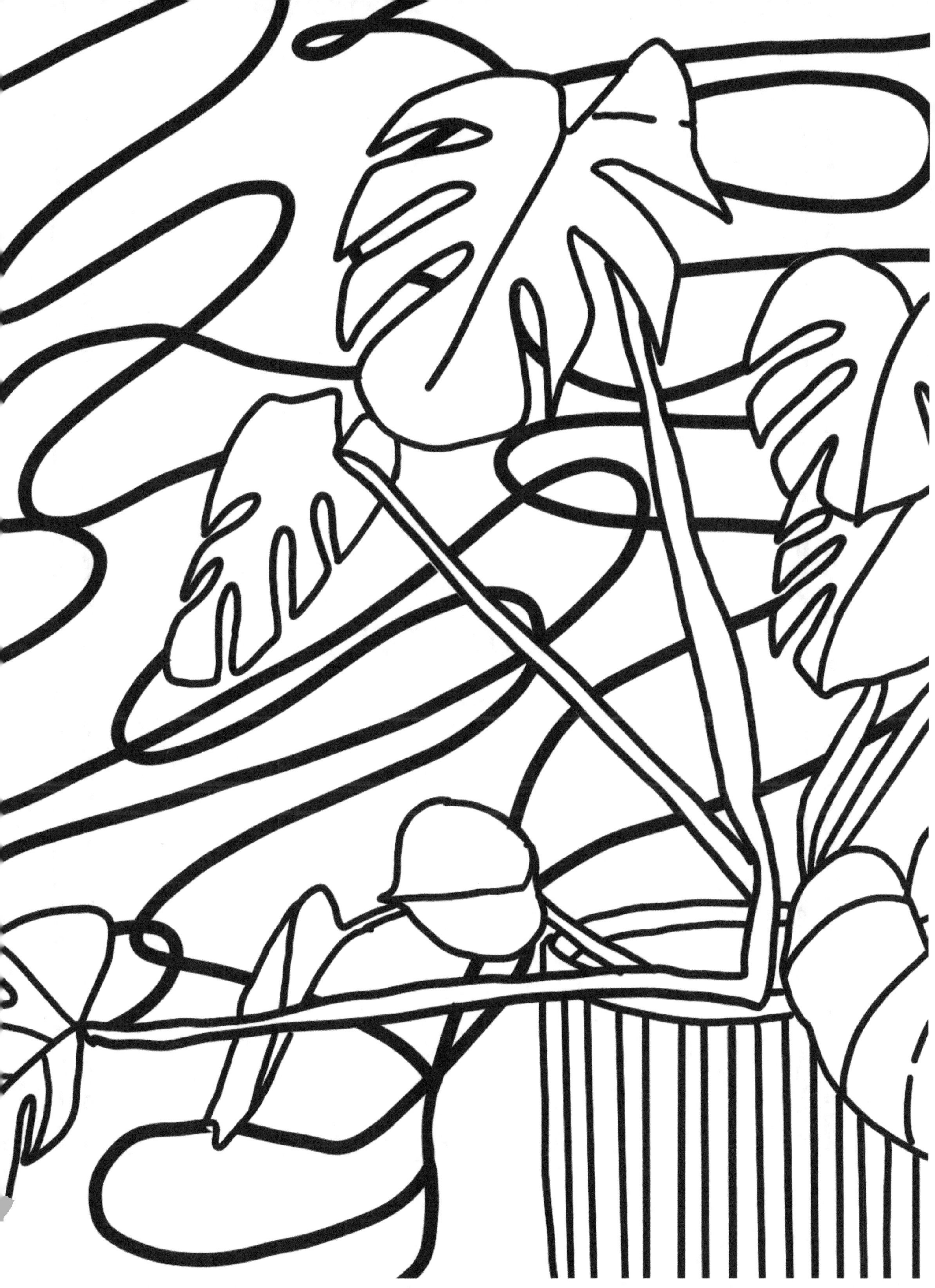

I matter

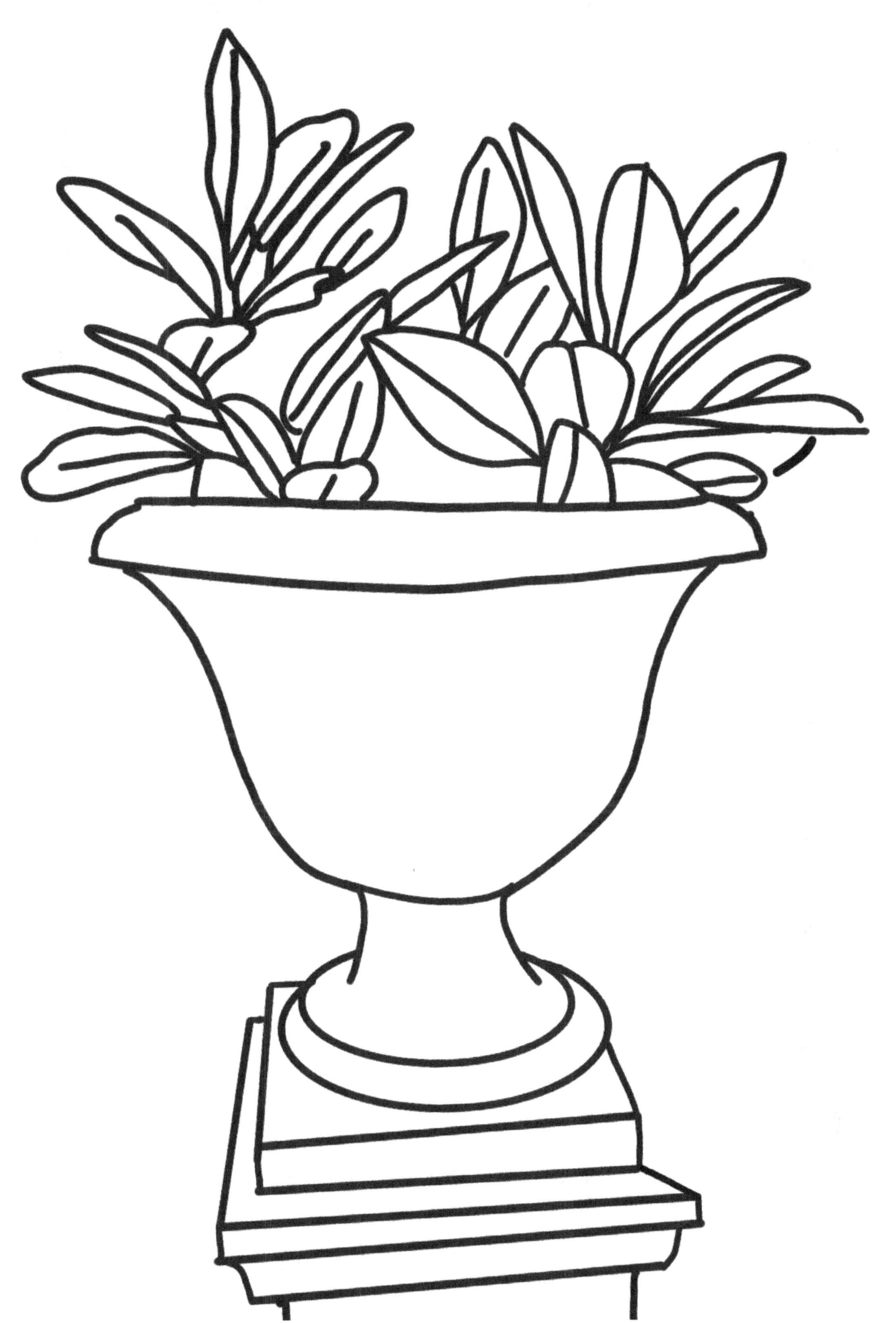

I do not have to be perfect

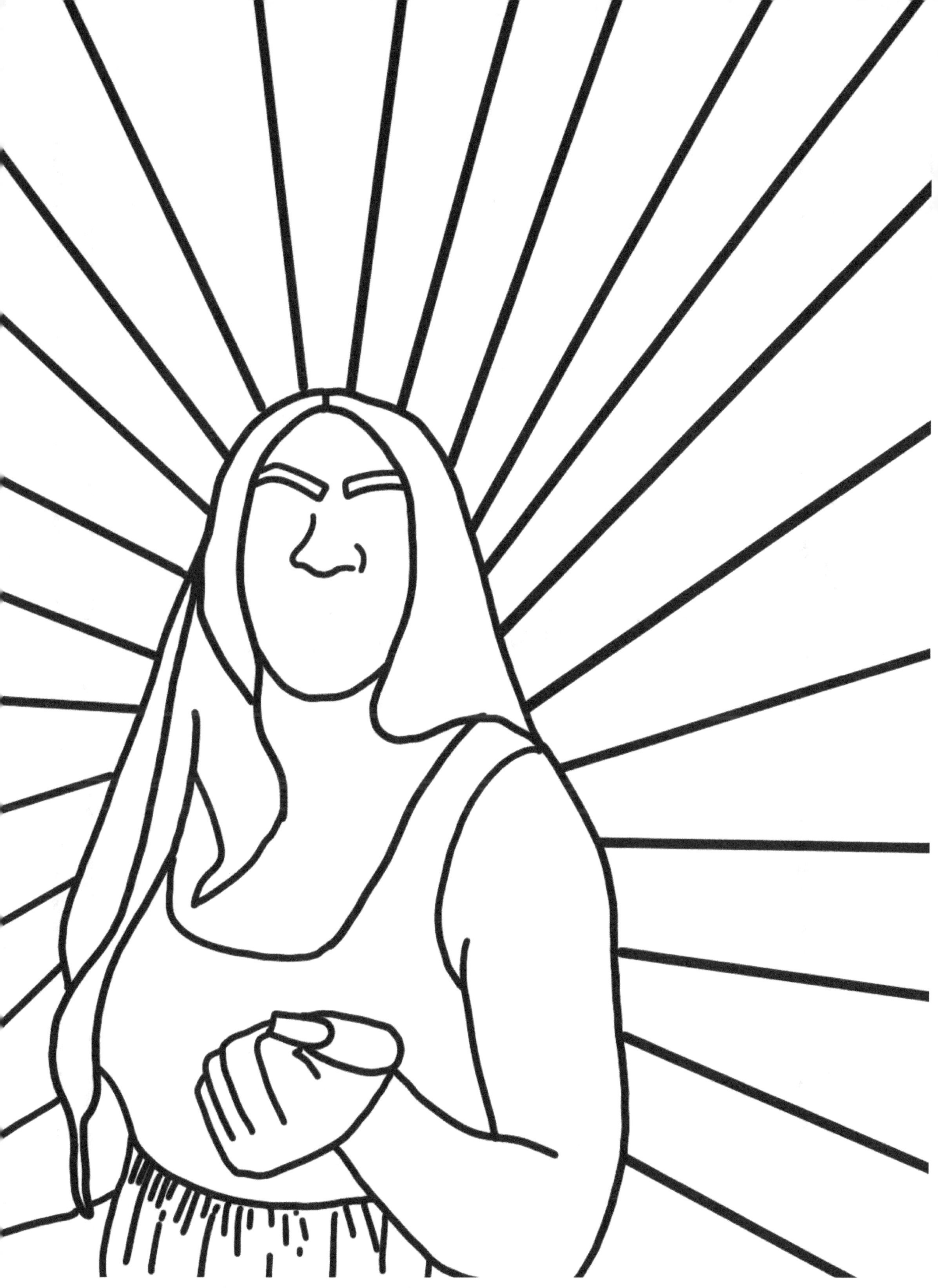

I deserve to be loved

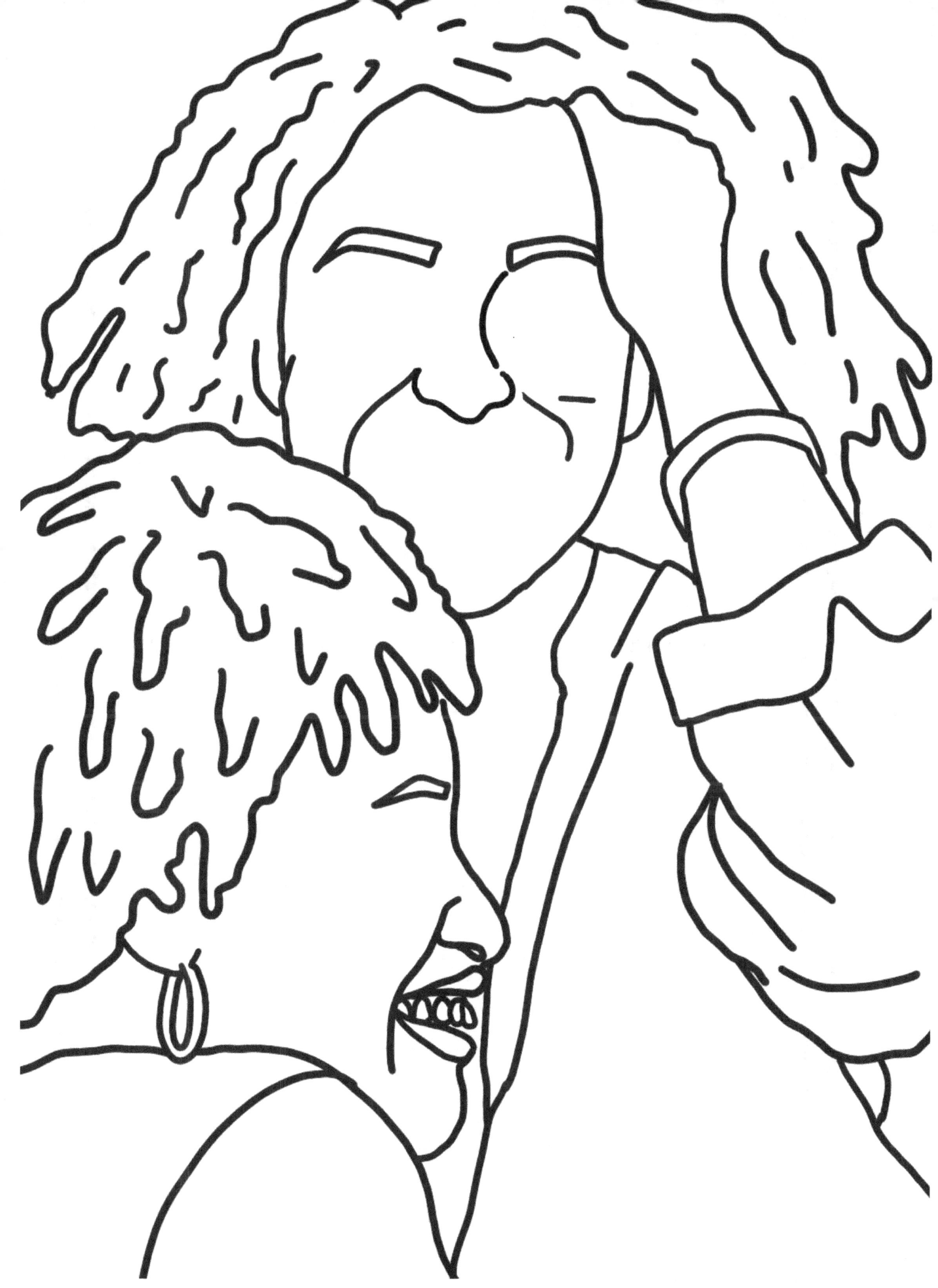

I can achieve all of my goals

YOU ARE THE FUTURE

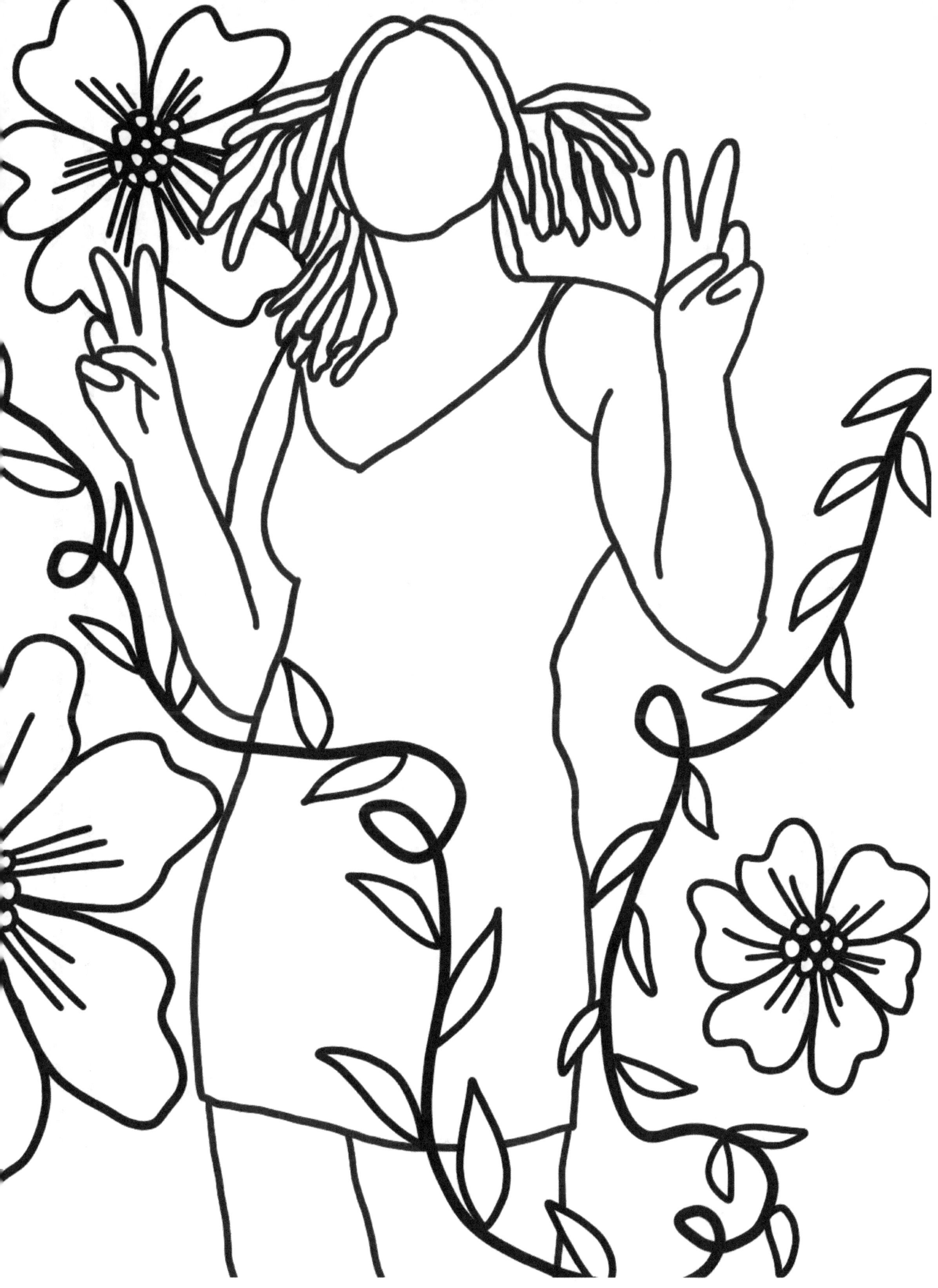

I have people who believe in
me

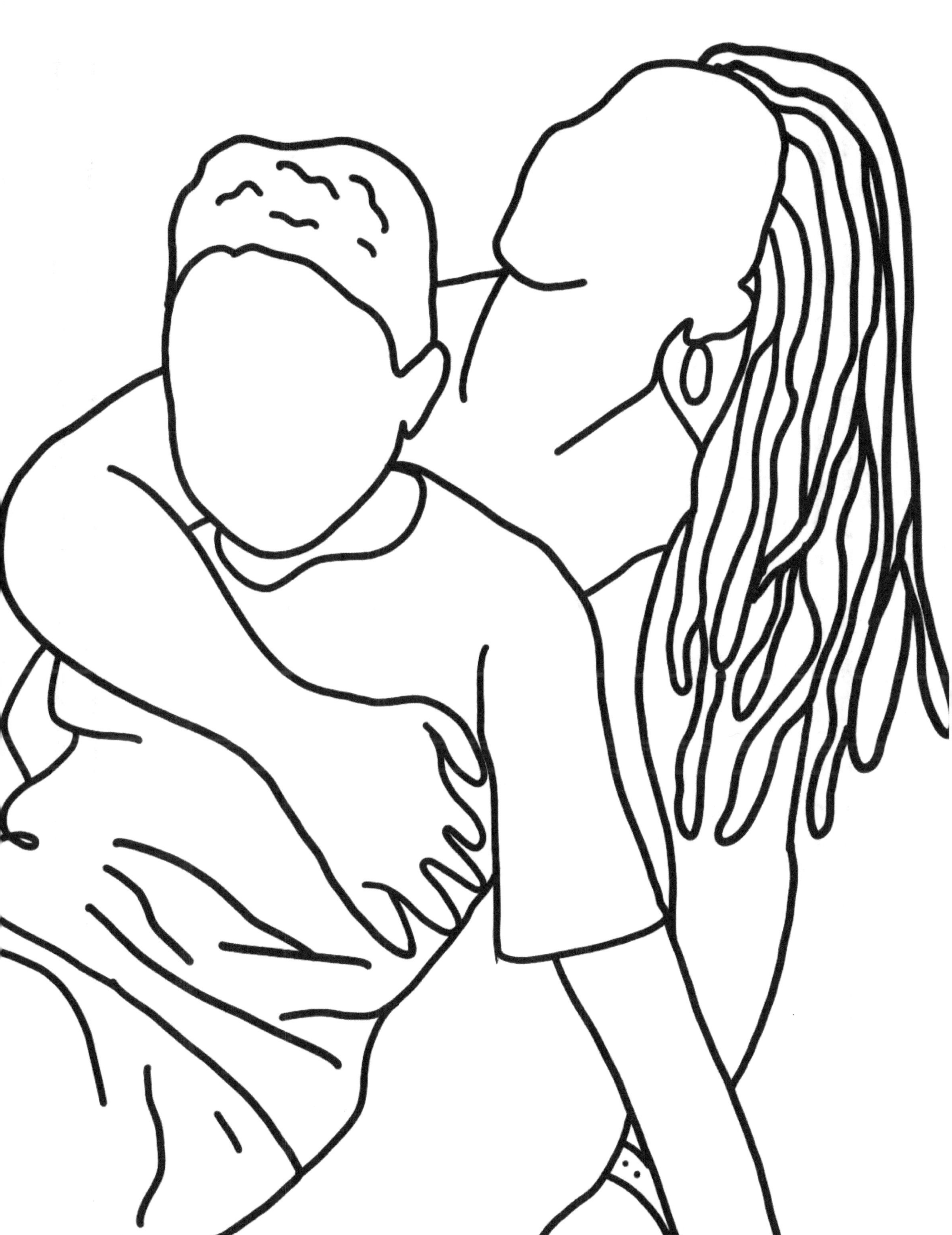

I believe in me

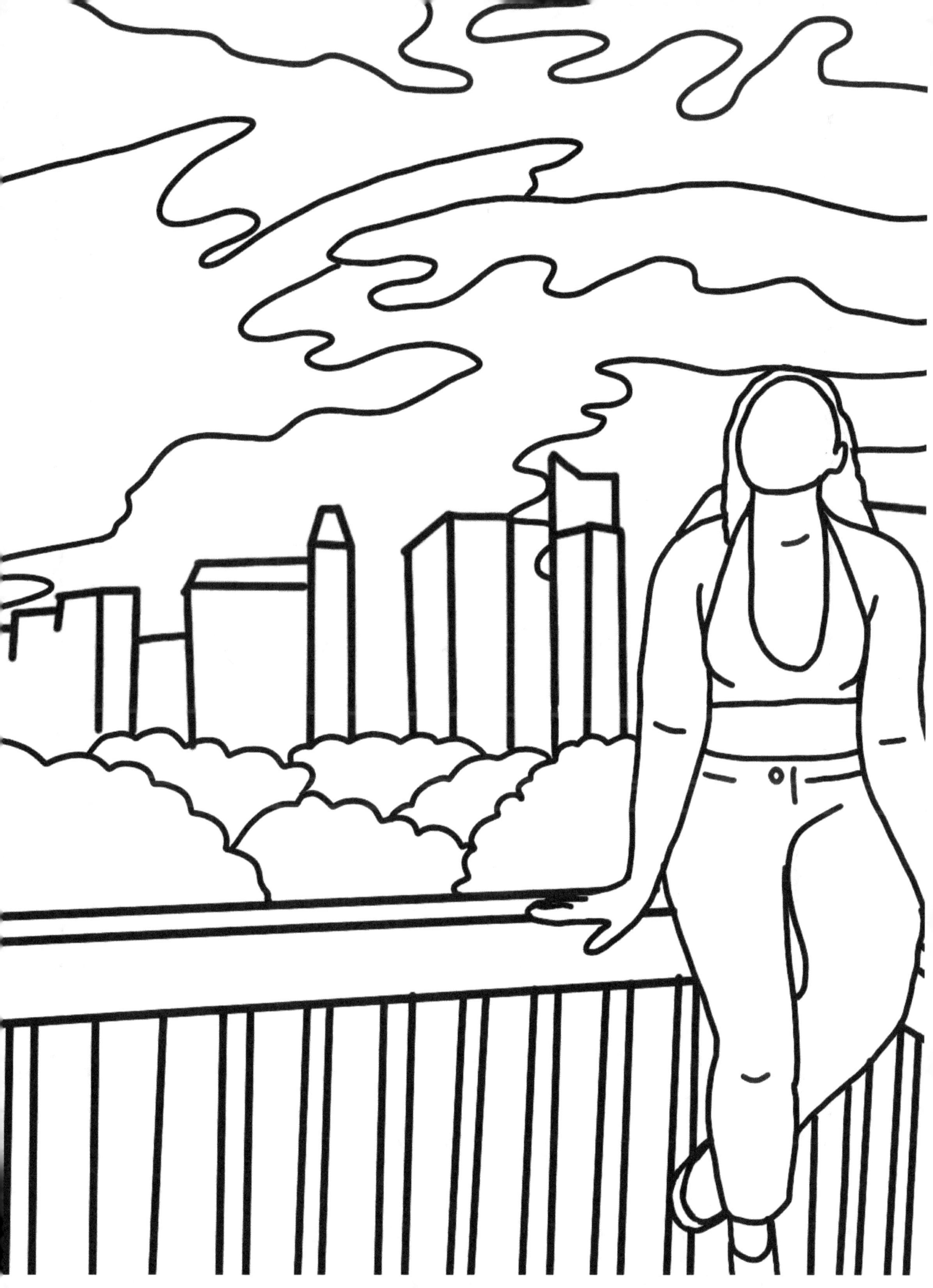

I am capable of doing good

YOU ARE THE FUTURE

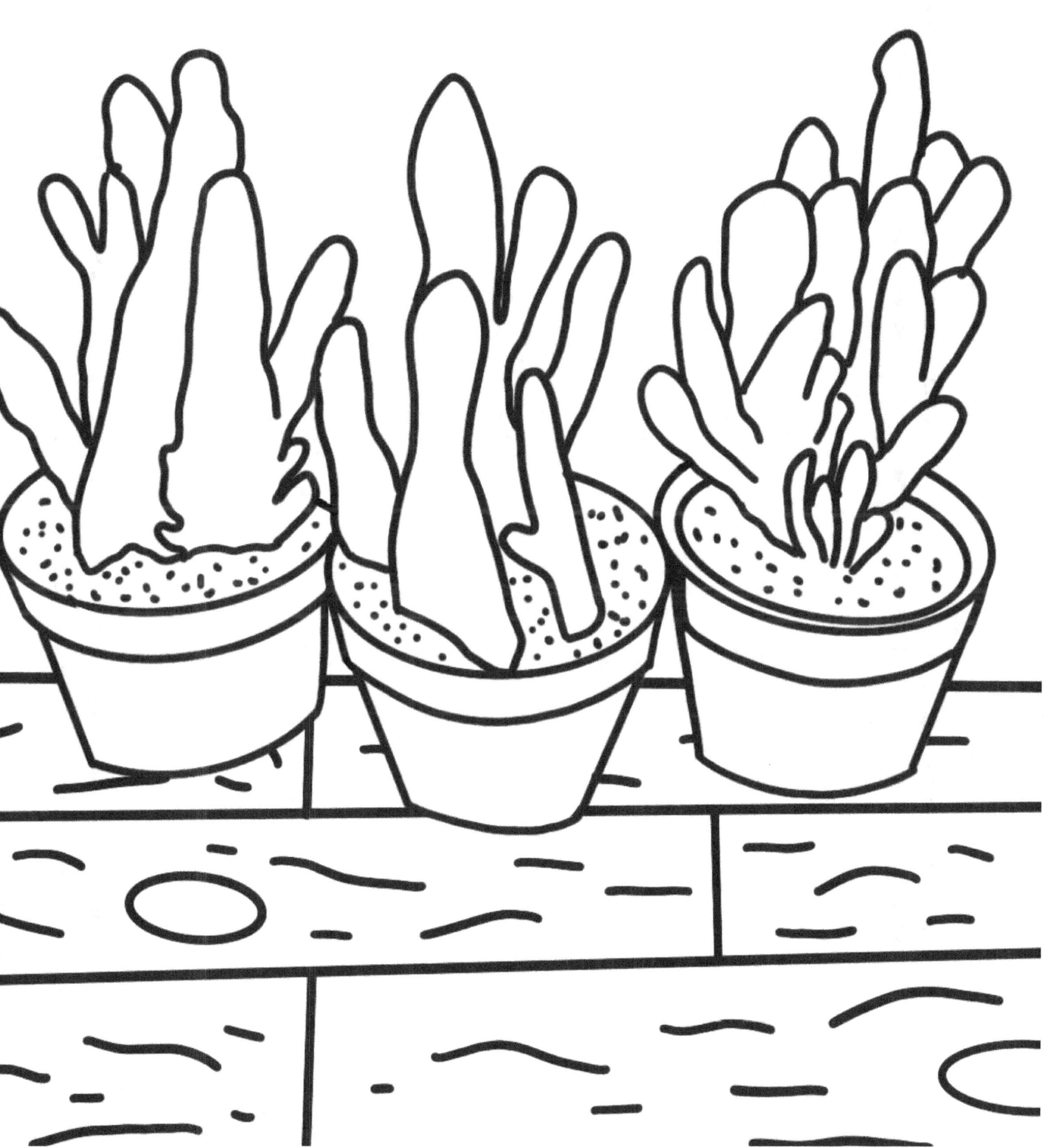

I am deserving of good

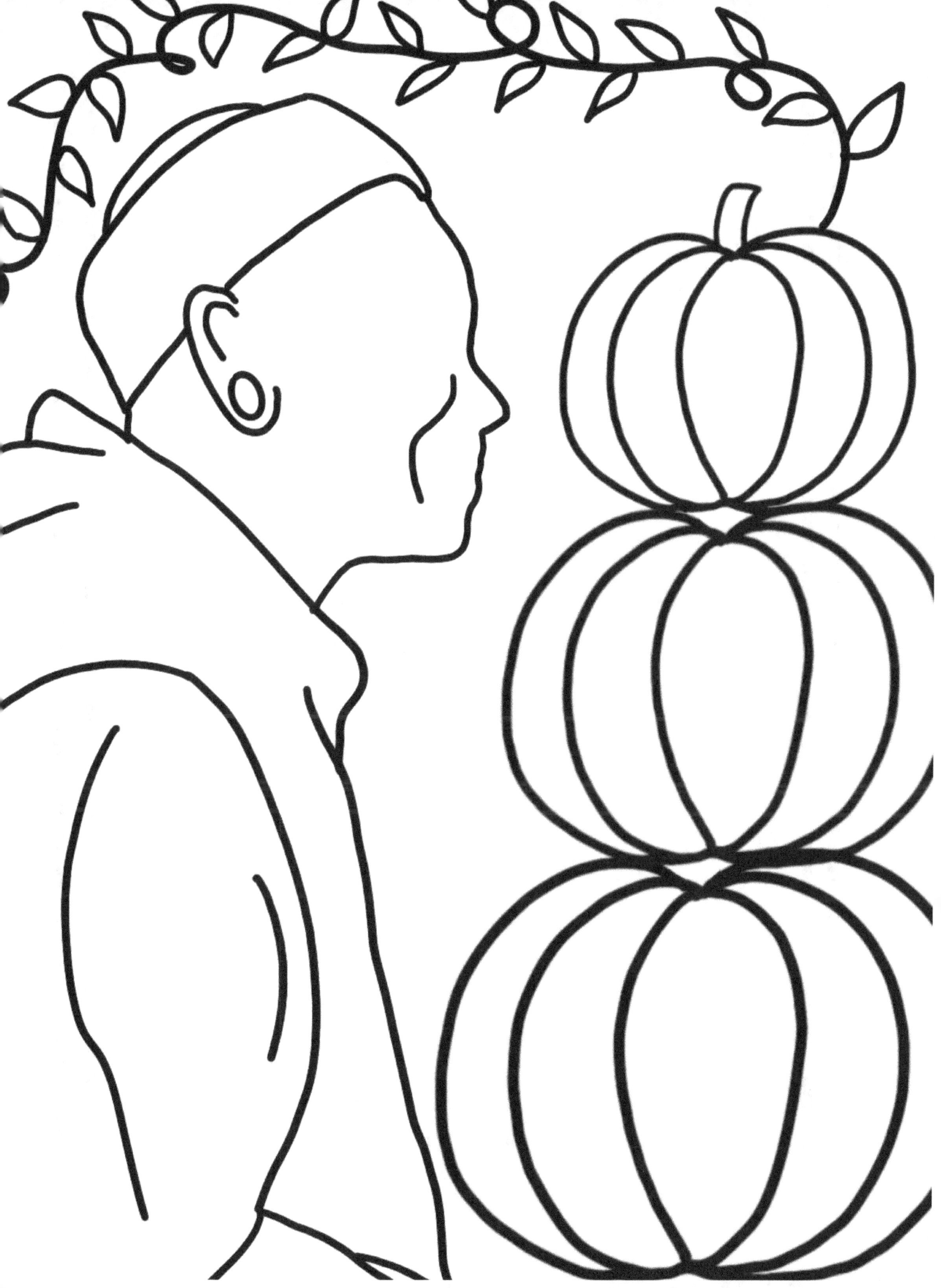

I am smart

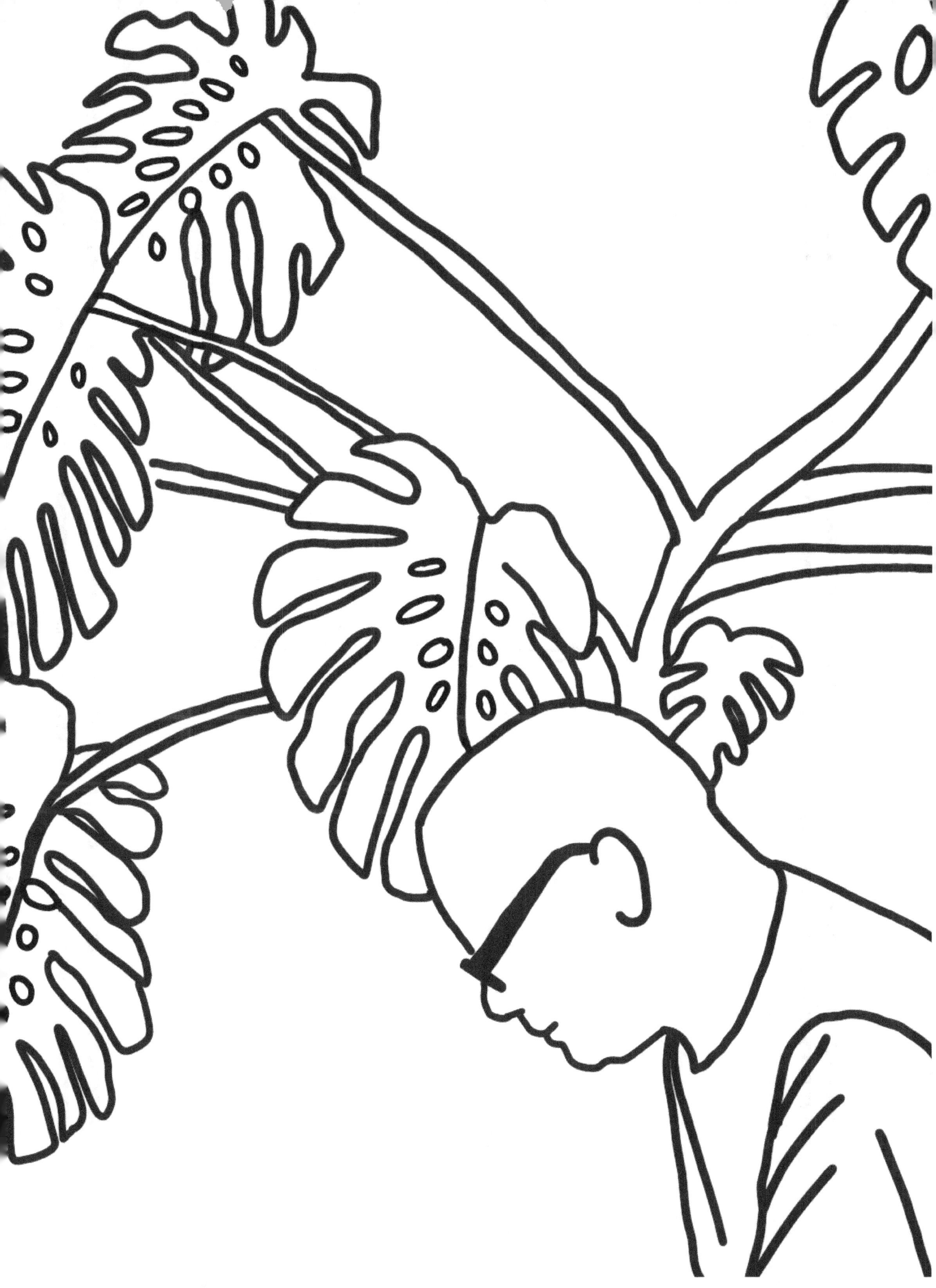

My opinions matter

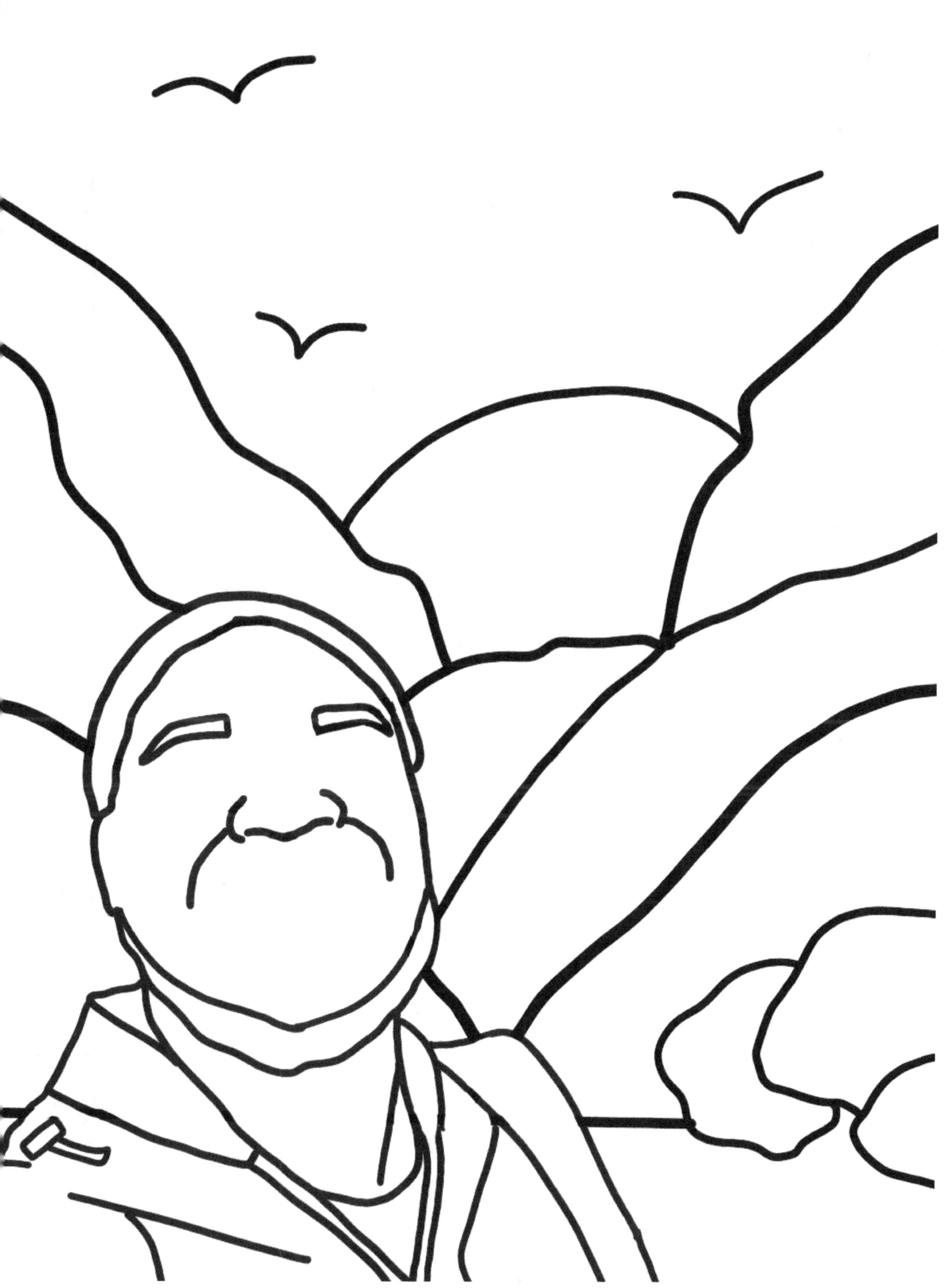

My feelings matter

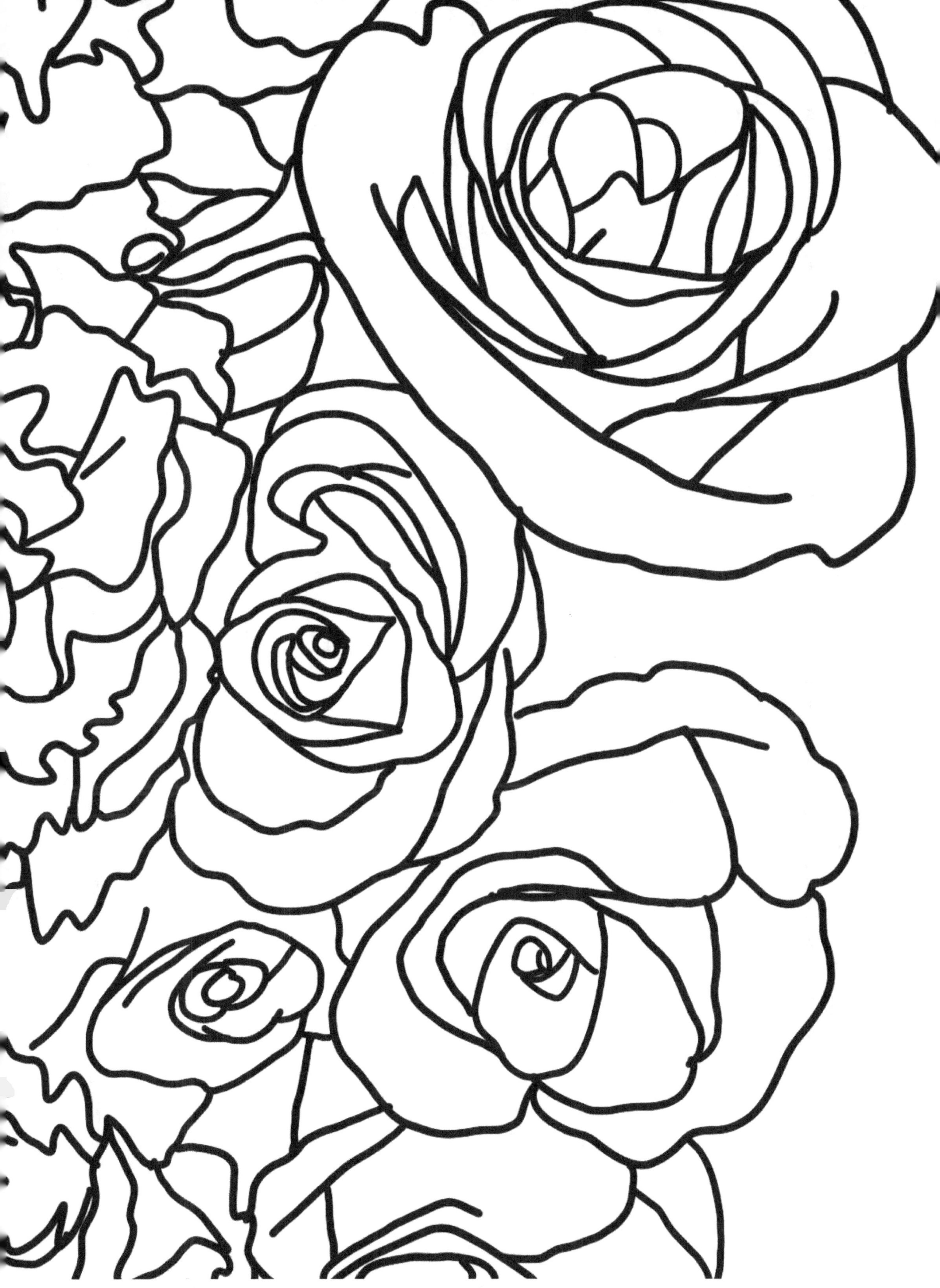

My dreams matter

YOU ARE THE FUTURE

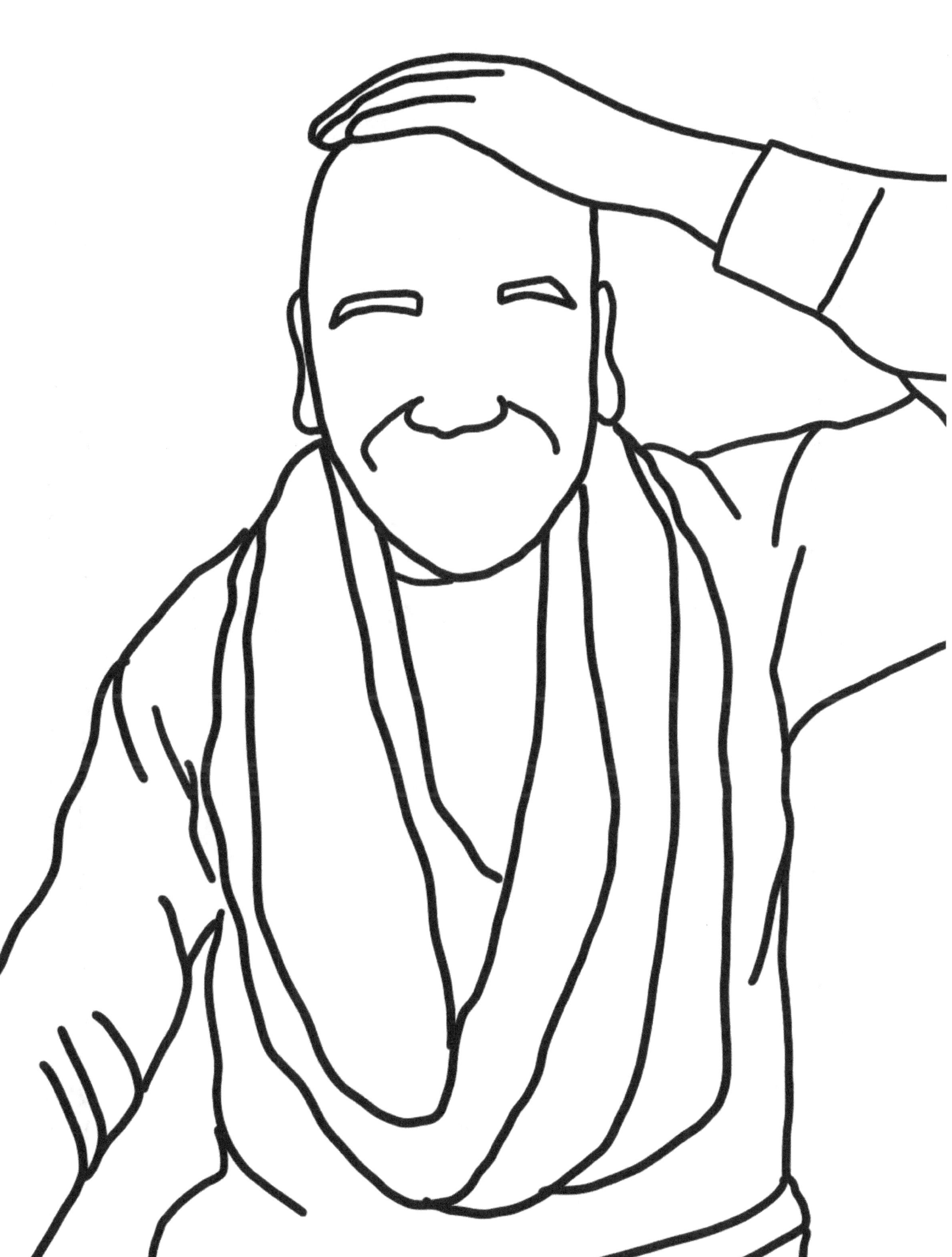

What are my dreams?

What are my dreams?

Use your imagination!

Keep this book til the end of the year. Review this book whenever you feel sad or down, especially when you have some days that are harder than others. Know that I believe in you and the people around you believe in you. When you need a reminder of your greatness, your intelligence, or the belief that you can do good, read this book and remember your dreams.

I believe in you and you are loved! Don't ever forget that.

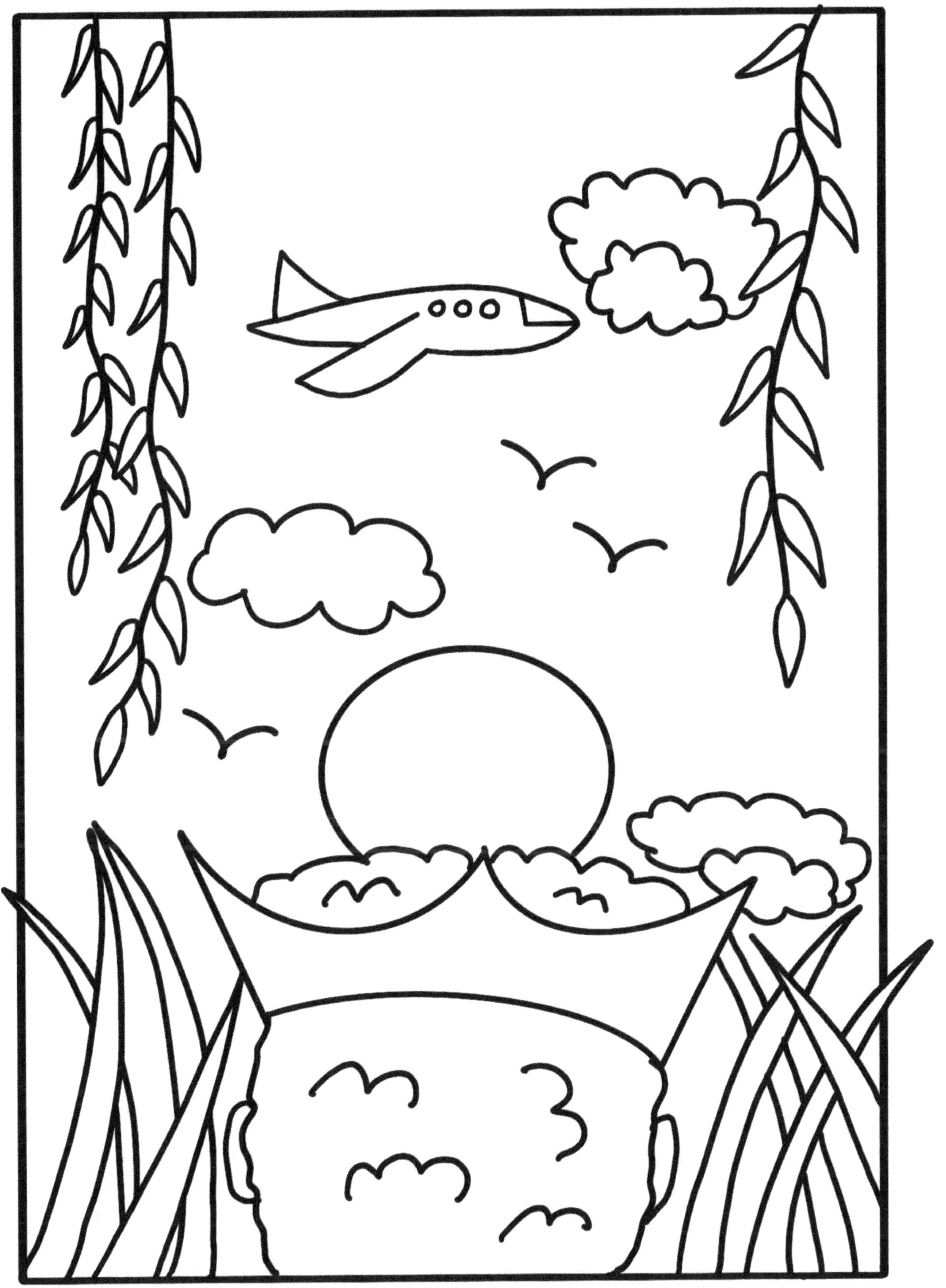

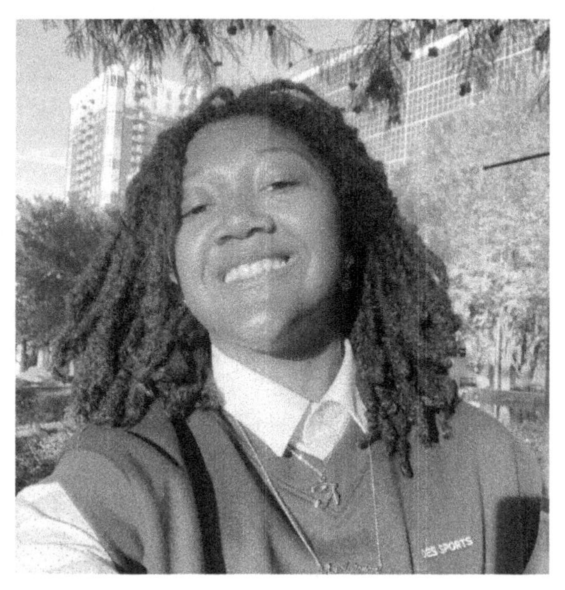

Creative Representation as a Movement for Change

Naomi Winston

For the past 3 years of my life, I have been designing coloring books. In doing so I have found a lot of myself, my passion, and my love represented in my work doing my best to spread love to kids like you.

I have learned a lot of hard lessons the past few years and I am so thankful to be able to encourage those of you to keep going. Sometimes life is hard, sometimes it isn't fair and sometimes things don't go our way. Imperfection, failure, and shortcomings are okay!

You are so capable of achieving your goals and I am incredibly proud to know you. I cannot wait to see the things that you will accomplish in the next year.

You are loved. You matter. You are everything you need to be.

Remember, everything has a purpose and you are everything,

We would love to hear from you!

Email letters telling us about your passion/dreams, comments, and pictures of finished coloring pages to:

 letterstotheauthor@revolutionaryheartsind.com.

We know that creating representation for Black and Brown kids means listening to their experiences, their stories, and their passions.

We would love to feature your artwork/stories!

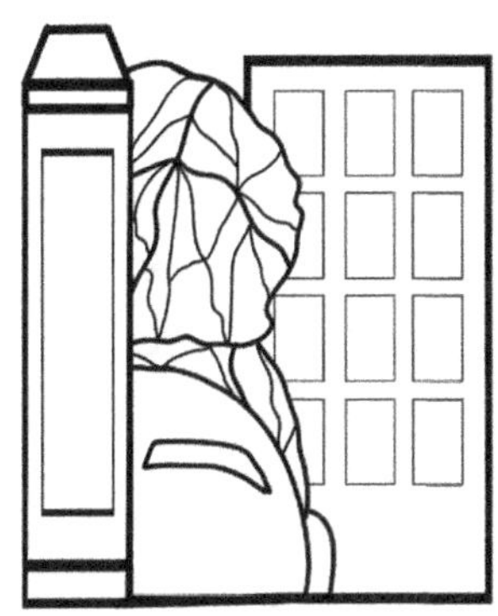

If you are interested in checking out our other coloring books make sure to go to
www.revolutionaryheartsind.com